FOR GOD ALONE

The Lives of the Early English Saints:
St. Hilda and St. Elfleda of Whitby

Front cover image: Window depicting St. Hilda at the Bailiffgate Museum, Northumberland.

Published by Leonine Publishers LLC
Phoenix, Arizona
USA

ISBN-13: 978-1-942190-28-8

Library of Congress Control Number: 2016951484

Printed in the United States of America
10 9 8 7 6 5 4 3 2 1

Visit us online at www.leoninepublishers.com
For more information: info@leoninepublishers.com

FOR GOD ALONE

The Lives of the Early English Saints:
St. Hilda and St. Elfleda of Whitby

H. E. Brown

LEONINE PUBLISHERS
PHOENIX, ARIZONA

Dedicated
to
St. Bede the Venerable

Contents

Preface

The lives of the early English saints, Hilda and Elfleda, are not very well known. The accounts and records that tell about them are not readily available. In order that Sts. Hilda and Elfleda can be better known, information on them from various sources—books, including dictionaries and guides, as well as encyclopedia, and Web sources—have been compiled together in this work.

The information on the lives, *per se*, of Sts. Hilda and Elfleda are placed in chronological order and are based strictly on the following source(s): for the life, *per se*, of St. Hilda, the Ven. St. Bede's *Ecclesiastical History of the English Nation*, especially chapter 23, which is entirely dedicated to her; for the life, *per se*, of St. Elfleda, the latter work, as well as the Ven. St. Bede's *Life and Miracles of St. Cuthbert*. Sources of information on their lives, *per se*, that are not mentioned by Bede are cited in this work.

St. Hilda, Patroness of Literature, as well as her pupil, St. Elfleda, have fittingly been given honor in many poems. Excerpts from some of these poems, as well as a full-length one, are included herein. Other than these inclusions, this work is by no means a literary work. It is, at best, a historical biography.

During the process of writing this work, which was over the course of twenty-some years, a complete record of the sources used was unfortunately not kept, but, as much as can be ascertained is contained in the Bibliography at the back of this book.

H. E. Brown
June 29, 2016
Feast of Sts. Peter and Paul

1

St. Hilda
Abbess of Streoneshalh (Whitby)
(614–680)

"all who knew her called her Mother"
Ven. St. Bede

It is well known, that, when Pope St. Gregory the Great saw Anglo-Saxon slaves in the Roman Forum, he, making a play with their name, called them, "Angels." But, he had also exclaimed, after inquiring the name of their king:

"Alleluias shall soon be sung in the land of King Aella."

Pope Gregory had thought of sending a mission to the "lands of King Aella"—the lands "north of the Humber" in England, the small kingdom of Northumbria (Northumberland)—then divided into the kingdoms of Bernicia and Deira. In AD 596, Gregory sent a mission with St. Augustine to the neighboring kingdom of Kent.

"King Aella" (560–588), whom Pope Gregory had noted, and who was known among his people as the "Man of Fire," was the first "king" of Deria. It was into King Aella's royal family that our saints, St. Hilda and St. Elfleda of Whitby, were born.

In the year 614, during the reign of King Ethelfrith the Cruel of Northumbria (604–616), who had usurped the throne of Deira, St. Hilda was born to Prince Hereric of Northumbria and Lady Breguswith. Hereric was the nephew of the son of Aella, King St. Edwin of Northumbria (616–633). Hilda's birthday is unknown. But, according to tradition, celebrated for a long time in Whitby, it is August 25 which is also the Feast of the Translation of her relics.

Hilda's name has different origins and meanings in Teutonic, Germanic, Old German, and Old Norse. In Saxon, "Hild" means "battle." The latter origin is probably the reason why there was a Saxon "goddess of war" called "Hilda." There are also the Anglo-Saxon "Hilda," meaning "a heroine," and Old German "Hilda," meaning "The Warrior Woman."

When Hilda was yet an infant, her father, Hereric, lived in exile, presumably under King Ceretic of Elmet (d. 616). Later, when King Edwin was restored to the Northumbrian throne in 616, he had Ceretic expelled, presumably for his part in Hereric's murder. Hereric's exile, probably, was in fear of the vengeance of the king, Ethelfrith. During the period of Hereric's exile, Hilda's mother, Breguswith, had a prophetic dream. She dreamt she was searching everywhere for her husband, but could not find him. After having exhausted her strength, she found a most precious jewel under her garment. When she looked upon the jewel with attention, it cast a light that seemed to spread throughout England. This dream was to come true, for Hereric was later "poisoned," and Hilda, whom the jewel represented, was to become a great saint, whose singular virtues were not only a source of edification to those who lived near her, but also to those who lived at a distance. "Her prudence was so great," says the Ven. St.

Bede, "that not only indifferent persons, but even kings and princes, as occasion offered, asked and received her advice."[1]

In 627, at the age of thirteen, Hilda embraced the Christian Faith, and the Ven. St. Bede says that she "preserved the same, undefiled till she attained to the sight of Him in heaven."[2] She had been brought to the Faith through the preaching of St. Palinius, first bishop of Northumbria. He had come from Kent with Ethelburga, the Christian queen of Northumbria. On Easter Sunday, April 12, Hilda was baptized along with King Edwin and many other members of his household in a small wooden church of St. Peter the Apostle in York. The king had hastily built this church while he was still a catechumen. Soon afterwards, he had a greater and more magnificent church built enclosing the prior one. Today this site marks the spot of "York Minister," one of England's greatest Cathedrals.

According to the Ven. St. Bede, from the time of her baptism, Hilda lived nineteen years "most nobly" in the secular life. She then resolved to serve "Him alone" in the religious life. "By despising the world for Christ, this saint became greater, even in the eyes of men, than royalty itself could have made her: but she was truly great only because the applause and veneration of this whole island was to her a most grievous persecution, the dangers of which alarmed her humble soul more than the threats of fire and sword could have done,"[3] so writes the notable hagiographer, Alban Butler. Hilda then left her native kingdom of Northumbria and went into the kingdom of the East Angles. From there,

---

[1] Bede, and David Knowles, *Bede's Ecclesiastical History of the English Nation* (London: Dent, 1963), https://archive.org/details/ecclesiasticalh00bedeuoft, 202.

[2] Ibid., 201.

[3] Alban Butler, *The Lives of the Fathers, Martyrs, and Other Principal Saints*, vol. 11 (Dublin: James Duffy, 1866), 309.

she desired to pass over into France in order to enter the monastery of Cale. Her elder sister, Queen St. Hereswith, mother to King Aldwulf of the East Angles (663–712), had entered this monastery. Hilda stayed there, probably, at the court of her nephew. However, at the end of a year, Bishop St. Aidan of Lindisfarne called her back to her kingdom. He gave her one hide[4] of land on the north bank of the River Wear (now the River Aire) where, for another year, she led a monastic life with a few companions.

Hilda was, afterwards, made abbess of the double monastery of Heruteu, "the Island of the Hart" (later called Hartlepool). There she spent about eight years establishing a "regular life" (*vita regularia*). It is unknown what this "life" was, but that it came from Iona. It most likely was a "rule of life" that was based on that of St. Columba of Iona. Aidan, who was from Iona, and others came and instructed her in this great task, seeing her innate wisdom and ardent devoutness to the service of God.

It was in the beginning of the last three years of Hilda's abbacy at the monastery of Heruteu, in the year 654, that St. Elfleda was born to the first king of united Northumbria (654–670), Oswy of Bernicia, and Queen St. Eanfleda, daughter of King St. Edwin of Northumbria. Princess Elfleda's name comes from the Old English *Æ_elflœd*, meaning "noble beauty" (*Æ_el* "noble" and *flœd* "beauty").

In 655, Oswy, in fulfillment of a vow he had made to God, if he were victorious in a battle against the heathen king, Penda of Mercia, dedicated Elfleda, hardly a year old, to our Lord in holy virginity. She was placed under the care of Hilda at Heruteu. Sir Cuthbert Sharp of Hartlepool's poem, "Saint Hilda," tells:

---

[4] A now obscure English unit of measurement that represents the amount of land sufficient to support a household.

Here did Northumbria's King perform
The vow to Heaven he made,
And consecrate, in victory's hour,
His infant Adelfled.[5]

Two years later, Hilda acquired ten hides of land in a place called Streoneshalh, meaning "Bay of the Lighthouse" or "Bay of (the) Light" (later called Whitby, meaning "White-bay" by the Danes). As a translated verse of the anonymous Latin poem, "St. Hilda of Whitby," puts it:

...Lighthouse Bay this prudent mistress sought, for there
She planned to stay: our Lady gave this place to her[6]

Hilda built at Streoneshalh a large monastery in the same manner as Monte Cassino, the first great abbey built a century earlier, after which no monastery was grander and more picturesque. Hilda's monastery was built on the summit of a rock, 300 feet above sea level, being surrounded by a bay. The name of the place probably originated due to the possibility that a third century Roman signal station[7] was once there, where signals could be sent either by semaphore, heliograph, or fire beacons; but it was significant due to the fact that Hilda's monastery was to become a beacon of light and peace for the souls of men.

Hilda established her monastery as a "double monastery" (*monasteria duplicia*), as did St. Hieu in 640 at the previous monastery Hilda governed, and St. Bridget around 480 at

---

[5] *The Whitby Repository, or Album of Local Literature*, New Series, vol. 1, no. 1 (Whitby: William King, 1867), http://books.google.com/books?id=hPgHAAAAQAAJ, 156.

[6] A.G. Rigg, *A History of Anglo-Latin Literature, 1066–1422* (Cambridge: Cambridge University Press, 1992), 23.

[7] "History of Whitby Abbey." English Heritage, accessed February 7, 2016, http://www.english-heritage.org.uk/visit/places/whitby-abbey/history/.

Kildare. In a double monastery, monks and nuns lived under the same roof, but in separate wings. The monks performed manual labor, provided the nuns with food, and most importantly, celebrated the Liturgy. Often, an abbess in a double monastery had the supreme rule over the monks as well as the nuns. This is said to have originated from Christ's words from the Cross, "Woman, behold thy son; Son, behold thy mother"; and that "maternity is a form of authority derived from nature, whilst that which is paternal is merely legal."[8] At that time, double monasteries were propagated widely by St. Columba and his followers and was common in Spain, Ireland, England, and especially in France, like those of Remiremont, Jouarre, Brie, Chelles, and Andelys.

Hilda likely took with her some of the monks and nuns from the monastery she had formally governed to her newly-built monastery. One of these was probably St. Oftfor, one of Hilda's five saintly monks who later became bishops, of whom the Ven. Bede says he "applied himself to the reading and observation of the Scriptures in both the monasteries of Hilda."[9] Another could have been the nun Begu, who had a vision of Hilda at her death and had at the time of her death, says the Ven. Bede, "served Him upwards of thirty years in monastical conversation."[10] Hilda also brought her charge, the Princess Elfleda, with her. It would be in Hilda's monastery that Elfleda, as soon as her age would allow, would

---

[8] Charles G. Herbermann, *The Catholic Encyclopedia: An international work of reference on the constitution, doctrine, discipline, and history of the Catholic Church*, vol. 10 (New York: The Encyclopedia Press, 1913), 452.

[9] Bede, 203.

[10] Bede, 204.

become Hilda's pupil and receive the habit. Sir Walter Scott tells in *Marmion* how many years later the

> …Whitby's nuns exulting told,
> …how in their convent-cell
> A Saxon princess once did dwell,
> The lovely Edelfled;[11]

Hilda became the founding abbess of her monastery and placed it under the same rule as the former. She taught those under her care to observe the virtues of justice, piety, chastity, and others; but above all, that of peace and charity. All things were held in common—none possessed any property. She also instructed them to devote themselves to much study of the Scriptures, which was in Latin (there was no Saxon translation at that time), as well as the performance of good works. As a consequence of this, many of the monks from her monastery were fit for holy orders. Five of them, in fact, became bishops, as well as saints. These were: St. Bosa, bishop of York; St. Hedda, bishop of Dorchester (Colchester); St. Oftfor, bishop of Wiccii (Worcester); St. Wilfrid II, bishop of York; and St. John, bishop of Hagulstad (Beverley), who ordained the Ven. St. Bede.

A humble, yet famous, protégé of Hilda's monastery was the first English poet, St. Caedmon. The aged herdsman, Caedmon, was ordered by Hilda, to recount to her a dream he had in which he had been given the gift of poetry, or as a translated verse of the anonymous Latin poem, "St. Hilda of Whitby," says, he had

> Then, though unwilling, Caedmon, called upon to sing,
> Produced such verses which he'd never known before.[12]

---

[11] Walter Scott and Michael MacMillan, *Scott's Marmion: A Tale of Flodden Field in Six Cantos* (London: Macmillan, 1899), 44.

[12] Rigg, 23.

Hilda also had him sing the Hymn he had sung during that dream which according to Bede went like this:

Now [we] must honour the guardian of heaven,
the might of the architect, and his purpose,
the work of the father of glory
as he, the eternal lord, established the beginning of wonders;
he first created for the children of men
heaven as a roof, the holy creator
Then the guardian of mankind,
the eternal lord, afterwards appointed the middle earth,
the lands for men, the Lord almighty.[13]

Copy of Cædmon's Hymn in the "Moore" manuscript (737).

After Caedmon had composed into prose a passage from sacred Scripture, he then, at the request of Hilda, entered the monastery. Hilda had also instructed that he be taught sacred history. It is for fostering Caedmon's gift of poetry that St. Hilda is the Patroness of Literature, particularly English, and education. Many schools and colleges in England carry her name.

Hilda's monastery became famous for its learning; its influence spread far and wide. A synod was convoked at Hilda's monastery in 664 to settle the question of Easter, the tonsure, and other ecclesiastical matters. The Scots held different customs from those who came from Kent and kept a different date for Easter. According to Eddi Stephen's *Life of St. Wilfrid*, the synod was held in the presence of Hilda. Hilda,

---

[13] "Cædmon's *Hymn*," Wikipedia, last modified July 4, 2016, http://en.wikipedia.org/wiki/C%C3%A6dmon's_Hymn.

having been instructed by Adian, was, along with her followers, on the side of the Scots. Yet, she accepted the decision of
the synod in favor of Rome and introduced the Roman prac-
tice in her monastery. Hilda was probably troubled, though,
with St. Wilfrid's (I) of York's part in it. For later, in 678,
she supported St. Theodore of Canterbury against him in the
division of the Northumbrian see and, along with Theodore,
sent messengers to accuse him before Pope Agatho. This inci-
dent was recorded a quarter of a century after it occurred, in
the year 705, in a pontifical rescript of Pope John VI, written
to the kings of Northumbria and Mercia, which is quoted by
Eddi Stephen in his *Life of St. Wilfrid.*

St. Hilda presiding at the synod of Whitby.

9

On November 17, 680, Hilda passed into the rewards of eternal life at the age of sixty-six. The Ven. St. Bede, in *The Ecclesiastical History of the English Nation*, gives a beautiful account of our saint's death, he writes:

> ...it pleased Him who has made such merciful provision for our salvation, to give her holy soul the trial of a long sickness, to the end that, according to the apostle's example, her virtue might be perfected in infirmity. Falling into a fever, she fell into a violent heat, and was afflicted with the same for six years continually; during all which time she never failed either to return thanks to her Maker, or publicly and privately to instruct the flock committed to her charge; for by her own example she admonished all persons to serve God dutifully in perfect health, and always to return thanks to Him in adversity, or bodily infirmity. In the seventh year of her sickness, the distemper turning inwards, she approached her last day, and about cockcrowing, having received the holy communion to further her on her way, and called together the servants of Christ that were within the same monastery, she admonished them to preserve evangelical peace among themselves, and with all others; and as she was making her speech, she joyfully saw death approaching, or if I may speak in the words of our Lord, passed from death to life.

> That same night it pleased Almighty God, by a manifest vision, to make known her death in another monastery, at a distance from hers, which she had built that same year, and is called Hackness. There was in that monastery, a certain nun called Begu, who, ...being then in the dormitory of the sisters, on a sudden heard the well-known sound of a bell in the air, which used to awake and call them to prayers, when any one of them was taken out of this world, and opening her eyes, as she thought, she saw the top of the house open, and a strong light pour in from above; looking earnestly upon that light, she

saw the soul of the aforesaid servant of God in that same light, attended and conducted to heaven by angels. Then awaking, and seeing the other sisters lying round about her, she perceived that what she had seen was either in a dream or a vision; and rising immediately in a great fright, she ran to the virgin who then presided in the monastery instead of the abbess, and whose name was Frigyth, and, with many tears and sighs, told her that the Abbess Hilda, mother of them all, had departed this life, and had in her sight ascended to eternal bliss, and to the company of the inhabitants of heaven, with a great light, and with angels conducting her. Frigyth having heard it, awoke all the sisters, and calling them to the church, admonished them to pray and sing psalms for her soul; which they did during that remainder of the night; and at break of day, the brothers came with news of her death, from the place where she had died. They answered that they knew it before, and then related how and when they had heard it, by which it appeared that her death had been revealed to them in a vision the very same hour that the others said she had died. Thus it was by Heaven happily ordained, that when some saw her departure out of this world, the others should be acquainted with her admittance into the spiritual life which is eternal. These monasteries are about thirteen miles distant from each other.

It is also reported, that her death was, in a vision, made known the same night to one of the holy virgins who loved her most passionately, in the same monastery where the said servant of God died. This nun saw her soul ascend to heaven in the company of angels; and this she declared, the very same hour that it happened, to those servants of Christ that were with her; and awakened them to pray for her soul, even before the rest of the congregation had heard of her death. The truth of which was known to the whole monastery in the morning. This same nun was at that time with some other servants of Christ, in the remotest part of the monastery.[14]

The Ven. St. Bede does not mention where St. Hilda was buried. But, it is most commonly believed, she was buried at Whitby.

During the invasions of the Danes in Northumbria, St. Hilda's relics were supposedly translated to Glastonbury by Abbot Tica, the last "Abbot" of St. Hilda's monastery, or by King Edmund I of England (939–946) when on his northern expedition in 944. But, this is according to William of Malmesbury's legendary history of Glastonbury. Dr. George Young gives a complete point by point refutation of this story in *A Picture of Whitby and Its Environs* where he concludes, "Upon the whole, we have reason to believe, that the bodies of Hilda, Elfleda, and other saints of Streoneshalh, slept there undisturbed during the period of its desolation, which lasted upwards of 200 years."[15] Another story is that King Edmund took them to Gloucester.

There is a Feast of the Translation of St. Hilda which occurs in the York Calendars under VIII Kal. September (August 25), "S. Hildae, virginis non martyris, [St. Hilda, virgin not a martyr,] III, lect." A Proper Mass and Office (see Appendix III) is assigned to it in the York Missal (Surtees Society, Vol. II) and York Breviary (Surtees Society, Vol. 71), I; Breviary I, Calendar after p. 726 (10). On this feast day of St. Hilda, there was an annual St. Hilda's Fair held on August 25, 26, and 27, at Whitby, probably in a place in Church Street called Fair-isle. It was granted by King Henry II of England in his "Charter of Grant and Confirmation to

---

[14] Bede, 204–205.

[15] George Young, *A Picture of Whitby and its Environs* (Whitby: R. Rodgers, 1821), http://books.google.com/books?id =Q4BHAAAAIAAJ, 82.

the Convent of Whitby," issued between the years 1174 and 1178, which read:

> Concedo etiam et confirmo praedictae Ecclesiae in eadem villa de Witebi...feriam ad festum S. Hildae, cum soca et saca, et tolle et team et infangenethef [Also I concede and confirm to the aforesaid Church in the said vill of Whitby...a fair on the feast of St. Hilda, with soc and sac, tol, team, and infangtheof]...[16]

It was confirmed by his successor, King Richard I. His confirmation read, "...we concede and confirm to the aforesaid Church...in the said vill of Whitby...a fair at the feast of S. Hilda, together with soc and sac,"[17] etc. An arbitration document, written in the fourteenth century by the Earl of Northumberland, Henry de Percy, mentions, "the Feast of the Translation of St. Hild, that is to say, the 25th day of August."[18]

The first monastery that St. Hilda governed in Hartlepool was destroyed by the Danes in 800. Excavations in 1833 (further ones made in 1838 and 1843) found the cemetery which belonged to it. Several skeletons, male and female, of a tall race with a great thickness of the forepart of their skulls, were found lying there. Above their heads were small stones of a very rare type—found in Yorkshire, Northumberland, and Ireland. They are marked with crosses, resembling Irish crosses of the same type. They also have inscriptions in Saxon, Romanesque, and Runic letters, exactly like those found in Irish manuscripts of the sixth and seventh centuries.

---

[16] J.C. Atkinson, *Memorials of Old Whitby; or, Historical gleanings from ancient Whitby records* (London: Macmillan and Co., 1894), 171 and 267. Author's combination of the Latin quote with that of the English translation.

[17] Ibid., 294.

[18] Ibid., Appendix B, 324.

One of these stones that was much larger than the rest, has an incised cross with the Greek letters, A Ω, in the upper limbs in the same manner as the Catacomb slabs at Rome; and an inscription in Runes, the name HILDITHRYTH. Fr. Daniel Henry Haigh identifies it as the tombstone of St. Hilda. He argues that Hildithryth was the full name of Hilda and gives some probable reasons for this. He also identifies the tombstones of her mother, Breguswith, and her sister, Hereswith.[19]

Whitby as it is today.

St. Hilda's monastery in Whitby was destroyed by the Danes in 867. The abbey still standing there today was built at a later period, c. 1078. *The Whitby Life of St. Gregory* mentions that in the church of St. Peter in St. Hilda's monastery, there was, besides the main altar, an altar to St. Peter

---

[19] Henry H. Howorth, *The Golden Days of the Early English Church*, vol. III (London: John Murray, 1917), Appendix I, 190.

and another one to St. Gregory. In the 1920s, excavations, in what was probably the nuns' wing of St. Hilda's monastery, found that it was built of wood and that there were many individual cells, each with a living room that had a hearth for a fire and a bedroom with a latrine. In one room was found "styli"—pointed instruments used for writing on wax tablets, as well as for pricking and ruling parchment, under-drawing, and hard-point annotation—also, pins and needles used for sewing, and a quern for grinding corn. In other rooms, there were loom-weights used for weaving cloth.

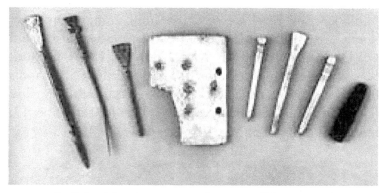

**Styli (writing instruments), most of them, used
at St. Hilda's monastery at Whitby and a tablet
hollowed out on one side to hold wax.**

Fifteen historic churches in England are dedicated to St. Hilda, eleven in Yorkshire, and two in Durham. In the town of Hinderwell (Hildas-well), nine miles from Whitby, in the churchyard of a church dedicated to St. Hilda, there is a beautifully clear, limpid, and abundant spring of pure water called, St. Hilda's Well or the Holy Well of St. Hilda. According to tradition, Hilda had a chapel here, belonging to her monastery in Whitby, where she retreated to during her life. After her death, the well was accounted, like herself, to possess remarkable virtue.

St. Hilda was not formally canonized, for there were no formal canonizations at that time. St. Hilda was canonized, as it was then done, by the voice of the local church. St. Hilda's *cultus* (cult) is attested very early. St. Hilda's name is in the Calendar of St. Willibrord, written in the beginning of the eighth century. It was strong in the North. Evesham kept St. Hilda's feast at a high rank because of its connection with the re-founding of Whitby as an abbey in the eleventh century. St. Hilda is not in Sarum, Hereford, or Roman Calendars. St. Hilda is commemorated on November 17 in the *Auctaria* in the *Usuardi Martyrologium* (Opera et studio J.B. Sollerii, *Acta Sanctorum*, Junii, Tom. vi. Parisiis et Romas, 1866); the Calendar of the Westminster Missal; and in a Durham Calendar (Br. Mus. Harl. MS. 1804); Gallican Martyrologies; and in a Durham Missal, "ad altare S. Johannis Baptistae et Margaretae ad IX altaria in eccl. cath. Dunelm. (Harleian MS., 5289). Her feast day is kept on November 17; translation, August 25.

The Holy Well of St. Hilda, Hinderwell Churchyard.

2

St. Elfleda
Abbess of Streoneshalh (Whitby)
(654–714)

"a venerable Handmaid of Christ"
Ven. St. Bede

After the death of St. Hilda, her devout scholar, Princess St. Elfleda, together with her mother, Queen St. Eanfleda of Northumbria, succeeded her as joint abbesses of Streoneshalh (at least until the latter's death, c. 700). Elfleda's mother had entered the monastery at the death of her husband, King Oswy, ten years before St. Hilda's death in 670.

Under Elfleda's abbacy, Trumwine, bishop of the Picts, took refuge at Streoneshalh, after King Egfrid of Northumbria was slain by the Picts in 685. The Ven. St. Bede says that Elfleda "found in him extraordinary assistance in governing, and a comfort to herself."[20] Following this in the same year, it is told in Conchubranus' *Vita Sanctae Monennae* (*Life of St. Monenna*), written in the first half of the twelfth century, that the Irish princess, St. Monenna, abbess of a monastery

---

[20] Bede, 213.

in Faughart, Ireland, went to "Villa quas vocatur Streneshalc [The vill that is called Streneshalc],"[21] where she met with Egfrid's successor, King Alfrid, who invited her to stay at the monastery. The king entrusted Elfleda to Monenna for instruction. Monenna stayed at the monastery for the span of about three years. In about the year 705, the first *Vita* of Pope St. Gregory the Great was written at Streoneshalh in Latin by an unknown monk of the monastery. It is mentioned in this *Vita* that, probably shortly before it was written, a South Anglian priest and monk called Trimma, had brought the remains of the king, St. Edwin, to Streoneshalh after a certain priest had appeared to him in a vision, saying, "Go to the place which is in the district called Hatfield, where Edwin was killed, and remove his bones thence and take them to 'Streuneshalac' (sic), which is the monastery of the most famous Elfleda."[22] St. John of Beverley was still a monk at Streoneshalh and was undoubtedly instructed by Elfleda.

Elfleda was a close friend, or as the Ven. St. Bede says, "was inspired with much love towards the holy man of God"[23] St. Cuthbert of Lindisfarne. Once, it is related, by the Ven. St. Bede, that Elfleda became very ill, so much so, that she almost was at the point of death and all the physicians' efforts were in vain. Yet, by Divine Grace, she gradually recovered her health, but not fully. The pain she had inside herself went away. She also regained the strength of her limbs. But, she still was unable to walk or stand because her feet would not support her. She could not move from place to place, except on all fours. This left her with great sorrow and the Ven. St. Bede says, "she never expected to recover from her weakness,

---

[21] S. Baring-Gould, *The Lives of the Saints*, vol. 7 (London: John Nimmo, 1898), 151, footnote 1.

[22] Henry H. Howorth, 200.

[23] Bede, 318.

for she had long abandoned all hope from the physicians."[24] One day, though, she turned her thoughts to Cuthbert and expressed her desire to have something belonging to him, "for I know, and am confident," she said, "that I should soon be well."[25] A person, soon afterwards, came with a linen girdle from Cuthbert. She was full of joy on receiving the gift, and understood that her desire had been revealed by heaven to the saint. She put it on. In the morning of the next day, she was able to stand on her feet; two days later, perfect health was restored to her.

About the year 684, Cuthbert had "confined himself within his own wall and trench and gave spiritual advice only through a window without ever stirring out of his cell. He could not however refuse an interview with the holy Abbess and royal virgin Elfleda."[26] She had requested him to meet her at Coquet Island, as she had some matters of importance to speak with him about. The Ven. St. Bede, in *Life and Miracles of St. Cuthbert,* gives an account of their conversation at this meeting, which shall be adapted here:

> When Elfleda had spoken to Cuthbert for awhile, in the middle of his conversation, she suddenly fell at his feet and begged him, in the terrible and sacred name of our heavenly King and of His angels, to tell her how long her brother, Egfrid, would live and govern the English nation. "For I know," she said, "that you abound in the spirit of prophecy, and that, if you are willing, you are able to tell me even this." He shuddered at this request yet, not willing to openly reveal the secret said, "It is a wonderful thing that you being a wise woman and skilled in sacred Scriptures, should call long the duration of human life:

---

[24] Ibid.

[25] Ibid.

[26] Alban Butler, *The Lives of the Fathers, Martyrs, and Other Principal Saints*, vol. 3 (Dublin: James Duffy, 1845), 200.

Copy of the Whitby anonymous life of St. Gregory the Great in the "St. Gall" manuscript (c. 9th century).

the Psalmist says, that 'our years shall perish like a spider's web,' and Solomon advises, that if a man shall live many years, and shall have been prosperous in all of these, he ought to remember the gloomy time of many days, which when it shall come, the past is convicted of folly; how much more then ought that man, whose life one year only is wanting, to be considered as having lived a short time when death stands at his door!"

Upon hearing this dreadful prophecy, Elfleda lamented it with many tears. After having wiped her face, with feminine boldness, she beseeched him by the majesty of the Holy One to tell her who would be the heir to the Kingdom, knowing that Egfrid had neither sons nor brothers. After a short silence, Cuthbert said, "Do not say that he is without heirs, for he shall have a successor, whom you will embrace like Egfrid himself with the affection of a sister."—"But," she said, "I beseech you to tell me where he may be found." He answered, "You behold this great and spacious sea, and how it abounds in islands. It is easy for God out of some of these to provide a person to reign over England." By this she understood that he referred to Alfrid, her illegitimate half-brother of her father, who on account of his love of literature was suffering a voluntary exile in Scotland.

Elfleda, knowing that Egfrid intended to make Cuthbert a bishop and wishing to know whither the effect would follow the intention, said to him, "Oh, with what various intentions are the hearts of men distracted! Some rejoice in having obtained riches, others always eager after them are still in want: but thou rejects the glory of the world, although it is offered thee; and although thou might obtain a bishopric, than which there is nothing more sublime on earth, yet thou prefers the recesses of thy desert to this rank;"—"But," said Cuthbert, "I know that I am not worthy of so high a rank; nevertheless, I cannot shun the judgment of the Supreme Ruler, who, if he decreed

St. Elfleda meeting St. Cuthbert on Coquet Island.

that I should subject myself to so great a burden, would, I believe, restore me after a moderate freedom, and perhaps after not more than two years would send me back to my former solitude and quiet."[27]

They then departed and returned back to their monasteries.

Elfleda again requested Cuthbert, after he was ordained a bishop, to speak with her and to consecrate a church at a monastery she had built, which, according to the *Anonymous Life* of St. Cuthbert, was at Ovington (now Easington). During their repast on this occasion, Cuthbert had a vision. Elfleda requested him, "I pray you, my lord bishop, tell me what you have just seen."[28] He told her he had just seen the soul of one of her holy monks being carried by angels to heaven. After she had asked him who it was, he said that *she* would tell him his name the next day while he celebrated Mass, which she did saying, "I pray, my lord bishop, remember in the mass my servant Hadwald."[29]

Elfleda, most probably, assisted in the burial of St. Cuthbert, or in the translation of his remains after his death. For one of the relics which were removed from his body in 1104 was described as "a linen cloth of a double texture which had enveloped the body of St. Cuthbert: Elfleda the Abbess had wrapped him up in it."[30]

Eddius Stephanus, in *Vita Sancti Wilfrithi,* calls Elfleda the comforter (*consolatrix*) of the whole province and a most excellent counselor (*optimaque consiliatrix*). He also tells how she used this gift of counsel in reconciling St. Wilfrid of York with St. Theodore of Canterbury, before the latter's death in 690, and with the Church in Northumbria. Theodore had

---

[27] Bede, 319–321. Author's adaptation of the text.
[28] Ibid., 331.
[29] Ibid., 332.
[30] Henry H. Howorth, 200.

written a letter to Elfleda requesting her to befriend Wilfrid, to which she most amply complied. In 705, when King Alfrid was mortally ill, she was present at his bedside and pleaded with him on behalf of St. Wilfrid. Later that same year at the synod at Nidd, she declared with a voice that sounded like it was from heaven: "Cease your discussion: I will declare to you my brother's last will, as I myself was present. He promised that if he recovered he would immediately obey the command of the Apostolic See and he is known to have charged the heir to do the same in the event of his death."[31] She ending by saying, "This, is the last will of Alfrid the king; I attest it before Christ."[32]

After having taken council with Elfleda, the synod made the decision to restore to Wilfrid all his former possessions both in Northumbria and Mercia, as well as his bishopric at Hexham and Ripon.

The last accomplishment of Elfleda, in record, is a written letter in Latin (see Appendix IV for the complete letter). It is the fifty-first, in the Collection of St. Boniface, probably given to Boniface during one of his trips to Rome. It is addressed to Abbess Addula of a monastery at Pfalzel (Palatiolum), daughter of King Dagobert II of Austrasia. In it, Elfleda entrusts to the care of this abbess another abbess, a spiritual daughter of hers from her youth, and consents to the latter's request to make a pilgrimage to Rome, to visit the tombs of Sts. Peter and Paul. It is signed, "Elfled, handmaiden of the ecclesiastical household."[33]

In the year 714, according to the Ven. St. Bede, Elfleda "departed to the nuptials and embraces of her heavenly

---

[31] Alban Butler, Herbert Thurston, and Donald Attwater, *Butler's Lives of the Saints* ([Tunbridge Wells]: Burns & Oates, 1956), 278.

[32] Charles Forbes Montalembert, 431.

[33] Matthew Hall, *Lives of the Queens of England Before the Norman Conquest* (Philadelphia: Blanchard and Lea, 1854), 245.

Bridegroom"[34] at the age of sixty and was buried at Streoneshalh, in the church of the holy Apostle Peter. The Ven. St. Bede does not mention the day of her passing.

During the reign of Henry I of England, St. Elfleda's relics were found, among the ruins of St. Hilda's monastery in Whitby, and translated to a place of honor in the church of the newly built abbey at Whitby, c. 1125. Part of her tomb, which was found in excavations in the 1920s, has her name, "AELFLEAEDA," inscribed on it.

St. Elfleda was so famous that her death is recorded in the Irish annals in the seventeenth century. St. Elfleda was canonized, as St. Hilda and all the saints in the Anglo-Saxon times were, by the popular voice (*vox pouli*). Her cult is attested only by late martyrologies. Both the Benedictine Monks' *Book of the Saints* (1921) and Richard Stanton's *A Menology of England and Wales* (1892) have St. Elfleda's feast day on February 14, but the latter, in the supplement of his work, says, "…perhaps the 8th February would be better than the 14th, as it has the sanction of some modern martyrologies."[35] St. Elfleda's feast day is commemorated on February 8 in Wilson's Martyrologe; first (W. i., 1608), and Wilson's Martyrologe; second (W. ii., 1640). Her feast day is kept on February 8.

---

[34] Bede, 144.

[35] Richard Stanton, *A Menology of England and Wales: or, Brief memorials of the ancient British and English saints, arranged according to the calendar, together with the martyrs of the 16th and 17th centuries* (London: Burns & Oates, 1892), 628.

Appendix I

Legends of St. Hilda

Since the time of St. Hilda, legends about her have been popularized in England. Some of these have been discredited. Like the one, popular among the country-folk, in which St. Hilda is said to have changed serpents into stones, when the town had been infested with them. Near Whitby Abbey there is found many stones having the appearance of serpents or snakes rolled up or in their coil, but without heads. According to geologists, these are fossils (molusca shells) called ammonites. They are found particularly in Whitby, where they are plentiful, and in almost every place where the alum rock is located. The scientific name for the ammonite genus, Hildoceras, was named after St. Hilda in 1876 by American zoologist and paleontologist, Alpheus Hyatt. Sir Walter Scott tells about this legend and another in *Marmion* (see Appendix II, for another poem, solely on this legend):

> …how, of thousand snakes, each one
> Was changed into a coil of stone.
> When Holy Hilda pray'd;
> Themselves, within their holy bound,
> Their stony folds had often found
> They told, how sea-fowl's pinions fail,
> As over Whitby's towers they sail,
> And, sinking down, with flutterings faint,
> They do their homage to the saint.[36]

---

[36] Walter Scott and Michael MacMillan, *Scott's Marmion: A Tale of Flodden Field in Six Cantos* (London: Macmillan, 1899), 44–45.

The other legend that Scott tells about in *Marmion* (the last four verses, in the quotation above) has also been discredited. In this legend the "sea-fowl[s]" mentioned are descendants of the wild geese which in another legend St. Hilda drove hundreds away that had long devastated the fields. According to naturalists, these wild geese in the winter fly in great flocks to the unfrozen lakes and rivers in the southern parts, like other migratory birds from across the sea. On their arrival at Whitby, they merely take a rest there, after their long flight.

The late Hilaire Belloc, who lived in England for most of his life, mentions yet another legend of St. Hilda in the beginning verse of his "Ballade to Our Lady of Czestochowa":

> Lady and Queen and Mystery manifold
> And very Regent of the untroubled sky,
> Whom in a dream Saint Hilda did behold
> And heard a Woodland music passing by:
> You will receive me when the clouds are high
> With evening and the sheep attain the fold.
> This is the Faith that I have held and hold,
> And this is that in which I mean to die.[37]

---

[37] "Ballade to Our Lady of Czestochowa," PoemHunter.com, last modified December 31, 2002, http://www.poemhunter.com/poem/ballade-to-our-lady-of-czestochowa/.

Appendix II

The following poem on St. Hilda is taken from: *The Whitby Repository, or Album of Local Literature*, New Series, vol. 1, no. 1, pp. 2–3 [See Bibliography].

Lady Hilda and the Snakes

Great grief was there in Streanshalh's cells,
For so the ancient story tells,
That Satan, hating much to see,
The peace and joy, where all agree,
The bliss of perfect purity,
And all the heaven of love;
Against this good the fiend rebels,
And seeks by dark, and hellish spells
To hurl his wrath 'gainst God above,
And on these holy maids, to prove
The power of hate, that in him swells.
With deep design, the Tempter plies
His every art, to gain the prize;
He whispers in the maidens' ears,
To some in hateful shapes, appears,
He seeks to light unholy fires,
And fan the flame of base desires,
He knows the weakness of each brother,
He knows how virtuous thoughts to smother
Some gasp and pant, through loss of breath,
Some pine in sickness nigh to death,
While others sleepless pass the night,

O'ercome with fear, till morning light.
They weep, they groan, they cry for peace,
But from their foes find no release.
Outside, the Convent, sad to say,
A host of snakes their poison play,
They spread through forest, and through field,
And efforts none, can make them yield,
The herdsman falls beside the cow,
The farmer faints behind the plough,
The sheep and horses poisoned lie,
While oxen stumble, groan and die—
And monks, and nuns do weep and sigh.
Sad is the heart of our good saint:
She fasts and prays, well nigh to faint.
No words of mine her grief can paint,
But Heaven her woe did see;
The tempter quits each holy maid,
He fled as Lady Hilda prayed,
    (Thus was it that the fiends affrayed
    From men possessed did flee,
    When Christ's great word "come out" they heard
    And owned the power of nature's Lord,
    And rushed into the sea.)
From out the Convent's quiet shade,
Then came the Abbess—pious maid;
A scourge in each fair hand she bore,
And drove the poisonous brood before,
But e'er they o'er the cliffs were crasht,
Off every one the head she lash'd;
Thus did the woes of Streanshalh cease,
And Satan broke no more its peace.
When many years were fled,
And oaks then young, were old or dead,
When abbey towers in ruin lay,

The sons of science came that way,
They said these shapes were not the snake,
But "just the shell their homes did make;
By instinct warned of danger nigh,
They snugly in their cells did lie,
And sinking into ocean's bed,
Long ages after, were found dead,
Their heads being there, as well as tails,
Thus science 'gainst traditions rails;
But not to me, this story tell,
Who from a child have known so well,
That every snake which strews the scar,
Was headless made by Hilda's lash,
When with her whip she smote, and far
Into the sea, them all did dash.

Appendix III

The following Mass and Offices of St. Hilda are taken from: *Yorkshire Archaeological Journal,* Vol XVII, pp. 46–49 [See Bibliography].

MASS OF ST. HILDA.

(York Missal, Surtees Society, Vol. II, pp. 91, 157.)

OF ST. HILDA, VIRGIN, viii Kal. Sept. (August 25).

Officium
(Introit).   ***Dilexisti.***   Thou hast loved righteousness and hated iniquity: therefore God, even thy God, hath anointed thee with the oil of gladness above thy fellows.

Oratio
(Collect).   ***Omnipotent sempiterne.***   O Almighty and Everlasting God, grant unto us that with fitting devotion we may rejoice in the feast of blessed Hilda Thy Virgin; that in her departure we may both praise Thy power and obtain the help provided for us, through Jesus Christ our Lord, Amen.

Or, as in one MS.,

Grant, we beseech Thee, Almighty God, that we who rejoice in the yearly solemnity of blessed Hilda Thy Virgin, may by her intercession be changed from that which is old into newness of life, through Jesus Christ our Lord, Amen.

Epistola

(Epistle).   ***Qui gloriatur.*** He that glorieth, let him glory in the Lord, *so* that I may present you as a chaste virgin to Christ (2 *Cor.*, x, ly–xi, 2).

Gradale

(Grail).   ***Dilexisti.*** V.   Thou   hast   loved righteousness, and hated iniquity. R. Therefore God, even thy God, hath anointed thee with the oil of gladness above thy fellows.

   Alleluia.

   V.   ***Emulor.***   For I am jealous over you with godly jealousy: for I have espoused you to one husband, that I may present you as a chaste virgin to Christ.

Evangelium

(Gospel).   ***Simile est,*** etc. The kingdom of heaven is like unto ten virgins, *so*, watch therefore, for ye know neither the day nor the hour when the Son of Man cometh (*St. Matth.* xxv, 1–13).

Offertorium

(Offertory).   ***Filiae regum.***   King's daughters shall be among Thine honourable women: upon Thy right hand did stand the queen in a vesture of gold, wrought about with divers colours.

Secreta

(Secret).   ***Hostias tibi.*** We offer before Thee, O Lord, this Thy sacrifice, that through the merits of the blessed virgin Hilda, we, being reconciled to Thy mercy, may be made a living sacrifice, acceptable unto Thee, through Jesus Christ our Lord.

   (So in one MS. Probably the Secret from the Mass of a Virgin not a Martyr was commonly used, as follows :—)

   Offerimus tibi.   We offer unto Thee, O Lord, prayers and gifts, rejoicing in honour of St. ***N.*** (Hilda); grant, we beseech Thee, that we may rightly do these things, and be able to obtain everlasting relief, through Jesus Christ our Lord.

Communio

(Communion). *Quinque prudentes.* The five wise virgins took oil in their vessels with their lamps, but at midnight there was a cry made, Behold, the bridegroom cometh, go ye out to meet Christ the Lord.

Post-communio

(Post-communion). *Caelestis convivii.* We beseech Thee, O Lord, that we, having received the blessing of this heavenly feast, may, by the intercession of the blessed virgin Hilda, and through that which is a sacrament to us, obtain the benefit of salvation, through Jesus Christ our Lord, Amen.

(So in one MS. Probably the Post-communion for a Virgin not a Martyr was commonly used, as follows :—)

Satiasti, Domine. O Lord, who hast nourished this Thy family by Thy sacred gifts, do Thou ever refresh us through the intervention of her whose solemnities we keep, through Jesus Christ our Lord, Amen.

NOTE.

It is, of course, to be borne in mind that the above passages from the Mass are only those which were "proper" for the day, corresponding to the Collect, Epistle, Gospel, and Proper Preface, in the English form of that service as contained in the Book of Common Prayer. The rest was very much as in the Roman Mass at the present time. The service (after the Introit, etc.) began with the *Kyrie*, which in the English service is lengthened and interspersed with the Commandments, then followed the *Gloria in Excelsis* when it was used, as it ordinarily was, then the Collect, etc., as above. After the Gospel, as in the English rite, came the Nicene Creed, then the Offertory. The Secret was said by the celebrant in an inaudible voice between the Offertory and the Preface, after which came the Prayer of Consecration and the Communion of the Priest. The "Communion" was afterwards sung or said, during the Communion of the people originally, and the Post-communion is a prayer implying that the people had communicated, as they formerly did at all celebrations, and as, in theory at least, they still may at any.

The whole service may be seen in English in Pearson's translation of the Sarum Missal, or, sufficiently for ordinary purposes, in "The Missal for the Laity," to be obtained at a small cost from the Roman Catholic booksellers.

OFFICES OF ST. HILDA.

(York Breviary, Surtees Society, 75, II, 507, 508.)

These were the ordinary Daily Offices with certain Proper Lessons, etc., for the day. They would be far too long to be given here as they stand, but they may be seen in the York Breviary, Surtees Society Edition, Psalter, Vol. I, cols. 27–944; Common of a Virgin, Vol. II, cols. 59–69; or in English, sufficiently well, in the Marquis of Bute's translation of the Roman Breviary, Vol. I, 1–178, and 878–886.

The only parts "proper" to St. Hilda are the three Proper Lessons, which are taken from Bede's *Eccl. Hist.*, IV, 23, and here follow in English.

OF ST. HILDA, VIRGIN.

The First Lesson.

Hilda the blessed handmaid of Christ was of noble birth, being the daughter of a nephew of King Hetwin (Edwin), named Hererich. With which king also she came to the preaching of the blessed Paulinus, the first bishop of the Northumbrians, and received the faith and sacraments of Christ. She then, having decided to forsake the secular habit and to serve Him alone, departed to the province of the East Angles. For she was a near relation of their king, and she had a desire to leave her fatherland and all that she had, and in some way to pass from thence into Gaul, and to lead the life of a stranger for the Lord's sake in the monastery of Chelles.

The Second Lesson.

For in the same monastery there was a sister of the same Hererich, the mother of Aldulf, King of the East Angles, subject to the regular discipline. Emulating her example, she herself also was retained for a whole year in the aforesaid province, with the intention of going abroad. Then, being recalled by Bishop Aidan to her own fatherland, she accepted the land of one family on the north side of the river Tigris[1], where for one year she led a monastic life with a few companions. After this she was made abbess in the monastery which is called Heorthen[2]. And when she had presided over this monastery for some years, it came to pass also that she undertook the government of a monastery in the place which is called Strenshale (Whitby).

---

[1] Mistake for Bede's reading *Uiuri*, of the Wear.
[2] Bede has *Heruteu*, now Hartlepool.

The Third Lesson.

But when she had presided over this monastery for many years, it pleased Him who hath made such merciful provision for our salvation, to make trial of her soul by long-standing infirmity of the flesh. Being plagued with fevers, indeed for six years she ceased not from her labours while enduring the same affliction. In the seventh year of her sickness she arrived at the last day, and about the cock-crowing, having received the *viaticum* of the all-holy Communion, amid words of prayer and exhortation, she, rejoicing, saw death; yea, she passed from death unto life, through Him who liveth and reigneth for ever and ever.

Amen.

The rest from the Common of one Virgin not a Martyr.

Appendix IV

The following letter of St. Elfleda is taken from: *Notes on the History of S. Begu & S. Hild: and on some relics of antiquity discovered in the sites of the religious establishments founded by them*, Appendix, p. 41 [See Bibliography].

AELFLAED TO ADOLANA

Domina sanctae atque a Deo honorabili Adolanae abbatissae, Elfleda ecclesiasticae familiae famula, sempiternae sospitatis salutem in Domino.

Ex quo nos formam vestrae Sanctitatis ab adventantibus ex illis partibas, rumore celebri referente cognovimus, inprimis nos vestram visceraliter, juxta praeceptum Dominicum, ex intimo pectore amorem cepisse, Domino dicente: Hoc est praeceptum meum, ut diligatis invicem; quapropter precibus subnixis suppliciter poscimus, ut sacrosanctis flammigerisque oraculis vestris nos apud almipotentem Dominum defendere dignemini, siquidem vobis vicem reddere nostra humilitas minime pigebit, apostolo Jacobo hoc ipsum praecipiente ac dicente: Orate pro invicem, ut salvemini. Insuper et summae Sanctitati vestrae ac solitae pietati N. devotam ancillam Dei, ac religiosam abbatissam, carissimam fidelissimamque filiam nostram ab annis adolescentiae, pro Christi caritate, et pro honore sanctorum apostolorum Petri videlicet et Pauli, ad ipsorum sancta limina ire cupientem, sed a nobis pro necessitate atque utilitate animarum sibi commissarum hactenus detentam, obnixe omni cum diligentia commendamos: et precamur, quatenus cum affectu verae caritatis in sinum clementiae piae a vobis suscipiatur cum his qui secum comitantur, ut diu desideratum ac saepe coeptum iter, Deo auxiliante, adnitente etiam vestra pietate, tandem aliquando perficere possit. Quam ob rem iterum iterumque repetendo petimus, ut cum vestris indiculis missisque ad almissimam urbcm Romam, prospero cursu, suffragante sancto ac signifero apostolorum principe Petro, dirigatur; et si quaudo praesens, Deo volente, adfuerit, quicquid viva voce, qualibet occasione stimulante, pro sui itineris necessitate suggesserit, paratum apud vos invenerit. Orantem pro nobis Sanctitatem vestram Divina gratia tueri dignetur.

(Ep. S. Bonifacii CLII.)

Bibliography

Books

Atkinson, J.C. *Memorials of Old Whitby; or, Historical gleanings from ancient Whitby records.* London: Macmillan and Co., 1894.

Baring-Gould, S. *The Lives of the Saints.* Vol. 7. London: John Nimmo, 1898.

———. *Vicar of Morwenstow.* New York: T. Whittaker, 1892.

Barrett, W.G. *Geological Facts; or, The crust of the earth, what it is, and what are its uses.* London: H. Hall, Virtue, 1855.

Bell, Arthur. *Lives and Legends of the English Bishops and Kings, mediaeval monks and other later saints.* London: George Bell and Sons, 1904.

Benedictine Monks, comp. *The Book of Saints: A dictionary of servants of God canonised by the Catholic Church.* London: Black, 1921.

Boutell, Charles. *Christian Monuments in England and Wales: An historical and descriptive sketch of the various classes of sepulchral monuments which have been in use in this country from about the era of the Norman conquest to the time of Edward the Fourth.* London: G. Bell, 1854.

Butler, Alban, Herbert Thurston, and Donald Attwater. *Butler's Lives of the Saints.* [Tunbridge Wells]: Burns & Oates, 1956.

Butler, Alban. *The Lives of the Fathers, Martyrs, and Other Principal Saints.* Volume 3. Dublin: James Duffy, 1845.

———. *The Lives of the Fathers, Martyrs, and Other Principal Saints.* Volume 11. Dublin: James Duffy, 1866.

Catholic Church, Richard Whitford, Francis Procter, E.S. Dewick, Christopher Wordsworth, and Wynkyn de Worde. *The martiloge in Englysshe after the vse of the chirche of Salisbury and as it is redde in Syon with addicyons.* Printed by Wynkyn de Worde in 1526. London: [Printed by Harrison and Sons], 1893.

Clemoes, Peter, Michael Lapidge, and Helmut Gneuss. *Learning and Literature in Anglo-Saxon England: Studies presented to Peter Clemoes on the occasion of his sixty-fifth birthday.* Cambridge [Cambridgeshire]: Cambridge University Press, 1985.

Colgrave, Bertram. *The Earliest Life of Gregory the Great.* Cambridge: Cambridge University Press, 1985.

Deanesly, Margaret. *The Pre-Conquest Church in England.* New York: Oxford University Press, 1961.

Deen, Edith. *Great Women of the Christian Faith.* New York: Harper and Row, 1959.

Fell, Charles, and Richard Challoner. *The Lives of Saints: Collected from Authentick Records of Church History.* Vol. I. London: T. Osborne, 1750.

Gasquet, Francis Aidan. *The Greater Abbeys of England: Illustrations in Colour after Warwich Goble.* London: 1908.

Grussi, A.M. *Chats on Christian Names.* Boston, Mass.: Stratford Co., 1925.

Gutch. *County Folk-Lore*. Vol. II. [S.l.]: David Nutt for the Folk-Lore Society, 1901.

Hall, Matthew. *Lives of the Queens of England Before the Norman Conquest*. Philadelphia: Blanchard and Lea, 1854.

Howitt, William. *Ruined Abbeys and Castles in Great Britain and Ireland*. Second Series. London: A.W. Bennett, 1864.

Howorth, Henry H. *The Golden Days of the Early English Church*. Vol. III. London: John Murray, 1917

Jewitt, Llewellynn Frederick William. *Half-hours Among Some English Antiquities*. London: Hardwicke and Bogue, 1877.

Jones, Thomas Rymer. *The Aquarian Naturalist: A manual for the sea-side*. London: J. Van Voorst, 1858.

Kay, Christian J., and Louise M. Sylvester. *Lexis and Texts in Early English: Studies presented to Jane Roberts*. Amsterdam: Rodopi, 2001.

Knowles, Leo. *Saints Who Spoke English*. St. Paul, Minn.: Carillon Books, 1979.

Lawrance, Hannah. *The History of Woman in England, and Her Influence on Society and Literature, from the Earliest Period*. Vol. 1. London: Henr. Colburn, 1843.

Lawton, George. *The Religious Houses of Yorkshire*. London: Simpkin & Co., 1853.

Lewis, Lionel Smithett. *Glastonbury, "The Mother of Saints": Her Saints, A.D. 37–1539*. Bristol: St. Stephen's Press, 1925.

Luce, Clare Boothe. *Saints for Now*. New York: Sheed & Ward, 1952.

MacMath, Fiona. *Saints' Names for Your Baby.* London: Marshall Pickering, 1997.

McAleavy, Tony. *Life in a Medieval Abbey.* New York, NY: Enchanted Lion Books, 2003.

Montalembert, Charles Forbes. *The Monks of the West from St. Benedict to St. Bernard.* Vol. II. Boston: Patrick-Donahoe, 1872.

O.S.B. *Virgin Saints of the Benedictine Order.* London: Catholic Truth Society, 1903.

Rigg, A.G. *A History of Anglo-Latin Literature, 1066–1422.* Cambridge: Cambridge University Press, 1992.

Sanderlin, George William, and Christopher Curtis. *St. Gregory the Great: Consul of God.* New York: Vision Books, 1964.

Scott, Walter, and Michael MacMillan. *Scott's Marmion: A Tale of Flodden Field in Six Cantos.* London: Macmillan, 1899.

Stanton, Richard. *A Menology of England and Wales: or, Brief memorials of the ancient British and English saints, arranged according to the calendar, together with the martyrs of the 16th and 17th centuries.* London: Burns & Oates, 1892.

Stodnick, Jacqueline A., and Renée Rebecca Trilling. *A Handbook of Anglo-Saxon Studies.* Hoboken: John Wiley, 2012.

Stoney, Constance. *Early Double Monasteries; A paper read before the Heretics' society on December 6th, 1914.* Cambridge: Deighton, Bell & Co., limited, 1915.

Walsh, James J. *These Splendid Sisters.* Freeport, N.Y.: Books for Libraries Press, 1970.

Wellan, T. and Co, and James Joseph Sheahan. *History and Topography of the City of York; and the North Riding of Yorkshire, embracing a general review of the early history of Great Britain, and a general history and description of the county of York.* Beverley: John Green, 1859.

Dictionaries

Benham, William. *The Dictionary of Religion: An encyclopedia of Christian and other religious doctrines, denominations, sects, heresies, ecclesiastical terms, history, biography, etc., etc.* London: Cassell, 1887.

David Hugh Farmer. *The Oxford Dictionary of Saints.* Oxford University Press, 2011.

Dunbar, Agnes B.C. *A Dictionary of Saintly Women.* Vol. 1. London: Bell, 1904.

Lewis, Samuel. *A Topographical Dictionary of England: Comprising the Several Counties…and the Islands of Guernsey, Jersey, and Man, with Historical and Statistical Descriptions; Illustrated…*Vol. 4, London: S. Lewis and Co., 1831.

Sheehan, Thomas W. *Dictionary of Patron Saints' Names.* Huntington, Ind.: Our Sunday Visitor, 2001.

Smith, William. *A Dictionary of Christian Biography, Literature, Sects and Doctrines: Being a continuation of "The Dictionary of the Bible."* Vol. 3. London: Murray, 1882.

Stephen, Leslie, and Sidney Lee. *Dictionary of National Biography.* Vol. 9. London: Smith, Elder, 1908.

Guides

Horne & Son. *Horne's Guide to Whitby, profusely illustrated: giving a detailed description of places of interest, streets, roads and footpaths in and around Whitby.* Whitby [North Yorkshire]: Horne & Son, 1897.

John Murray (Firm). *Handbook for Travellers in Yorkshire: With map and plans.* 1867.

John Murray (Firm), and Augustus J.C. Hare. *A Handbook for Travellers in Durham and Northumberland.* London: J. Murray, 1873.

Encyclopedias

Herbermann, Charles G. *The Catholic Encyclopedia: An international work of reference on the constitution, doctrine, discipline, and history of the Catholic Church.* Vol. 6. New York: The Encyclopedia Press, 1913.

———. *The Catholic Encyclopedia: An international work of reference on the constitution, doctrine, and history of the Catholic Church.* Vol. 7. New York: The Encyclopedia Press, 1913.

———. *The Catholic Encyclopedia: An international work of reference on the constitution, doctrine, discipline, and history of the Catholic Church.* Vol. 10. New York: The Encyclopedia Press, 1913.

Web Sources

"The Anglo-Saxon Chronicle." *Britannia Internet Magazine, LLC.* Accessed September 8, 2007. http://www.britannia.com/history/docs/asstart.html.

"Ballade to Our Lady of Czestochowa." PoemHunter.com. Last modified December 31, 2002. http://www.poemhunter.com/poem/ballade-to-our-lady-of-czestochowa/.

Baring-Gould, S. *Virgin Saints and Martyrs. With sixteen full-page illustrations.* London: Hutchison, 1900. https://books.google.com/books?id=XtRqmrSGas4C.

Bede, and David Knowles. *Bede's Ecclesiastical History of the English Nation.* London: Dent, 1963. https://archive.org/details/ecclesiasticalh00bedeuoft.

Buckingham, James Silk, John Sterling, Frederick Denison Maurice, Henry Stebbing, Charles Wentworth Dilke, Thomas Kibble Hervey, William Hepworth Dixon, Norman Maccoll, Vernon Horace Rendall, and John Middleton Murry. *The Athenaeum.* [S.l.]: W. Lewer, 1904. https://books.google.com/books?id=LDs6AQAAIAAJ.

Burnett, Tony. "Lines of Sight Through Craven." North Craven Heritage Trust. Accessed February 7, 2016. http://www.northcravenheritage.org.uk/nchtjournal/Journals/1999/J99A11.html.

"Elfleda." Behind the Name. Accessed December 4, 2007. http://www.behindthename.com/name/elfleda.

Haigh, Daniel H. *Notes on the History of S. Begu & S. Hild: and on some relics of antiquity discovered in the sites of the religious establishments founded by them.* Hartlepool: J. Procter, 1858. https://books.google.com/books?id=O_kGAAAAQAAJ.

"Hilda." Behind the Name. Accessed December 4, 2007. http://www.behindthename.com/name/hilda.

"History of Whitby Abbey." English Heritage. Accessed February 7, 2016. http://www.english-heritage.org.uk/visit/places/whitby-abbey/history/.

Jewitt, Llewellynn Frederick William. *The Reliquary: Quarterly archaeological journal and review: a depository for precious relics—legendary, biographical and historical: illustrative of the habits, customs, and pursuits, of our forefathers.* Vol. XVII. London: Bemrose & Sons, 1877. https://archive.org/details/reliquaryquarte01jewigoog.

Poole, Reginald L., ed. *The English Historical Review.* Vol. 35. London: Longmans, 1920. https://archive.org/details/englishhistorica35londuoft.

"St Hilda and the Kings of Northumbria." Queensland. Accessed June 19, 2000. http://www.queensland.co.uk/hilda.html.

"St Modwen." Ss Mary and Modwen. Accessed December 26, 2014. http://www.maryandmodwen.org.uk/st-modwen.html.

Sterling, William. "Anglo-Saxon Queens." William Sterling. Accessed February 7, 2016. http://www.williamsterling.co.uk/2011/06/anglo-saxon-queens/.

"Trinity College, Cambridge, MS O.9.38." Scriptorium: Medieval and Early Modern Manuscripts Online. Accessed August 26, 2015. http://scriptorium. english.cam.ac.uk/manuscripts/images/index. php?ms=O.9.38

United States Conference of Catholic Bishops Office of Media Relations. "Making Saints." Backgrounder. Accessed July 25, 2016. http://www.usccb.org/_cs_upload/8233_1.pdf.

The Whitby Repository, or Album of Local Literature. New Series. Vol. 1. No. 1. Whitby: William King, 1867. http://books.google.com/books?id=hPgHAAAAQAA.

Yorkshire Archaeological Society. *Yorkshire Archaeological Journal.* Vol 17. [S.l: s.n.], 1903. https://archive.org/details/yorkshirearchae17socigoog.

Young, George. *A Picture of Whitby and its Environs.* Whitby: R. Rodgers, 1821. http://books.google.com/books?id=Q4BHAAAAIAAJ.

About the Author

H.E. BROWN majored in music at her local community college and today continues self-study in liberal arts, with a concentration in philosophy and theology. Brown enjoys writing and her first work is *She Shall Crush Thy Head: Selected Writings of St. Maximilian Kolbe,* published by Leonine Publishers. She resides in Houston, Texas, with her family.

About Leonine Publishers

Leonine Publishers LLC makes fine Catholic literature available to Catholics throughout the English-speaking world. Leonine Publishers offers an innovative "hybrid" approach to book publication that helps authors as well as readers. Please visit our web site at www.leoninepublishers.com to learn more about us. Browse our online bookstore to find more solid Catholic titles to uplift, challenge, and inspire.

Our patron and namesake is Pope Leo XIII, a prudent, yet uncompromising pope during the stormy years at the close of the 19th century. Please join us as we ask his intercession for our family of readers and authors.

Do you have a book inside you? Visit our web site today. Leonine Publishers accepts manuscripts from Catholic authors like you. If your book is selected for publication, you will have an active part in the production process. This book is an example of our growing selection of literature for the busy Catholic reader of the 21st century.

www.leoninepublishers.com

CPSIA information can be obtained
at www.ICGtesting.com
Printed in the USA
LVHW040740120420
653129LV00031B/552